the backyard kids™

Undercover

Property of:

_____

If lost, please return to:

215 Bulldog Road, Somerville

Dear Fellow Backyard Kid,

A few of the original Backyard Kids created this awesome, undercover journal. We were tired of boring, smelly, same-old, school.

We were tired of our parents always yelling at us to, "Get off the electronics" and "Go read a book!"

BYK is short for Backyard Kids!!

💡 LIGHTBULB! 💡 Us BYK's got together and made a book that — LOOKS like a

book — **BUT** isn't really, truly a book.

We created something FUN!

A journal unlike the rest!

Guess What? After all that work, it turns out...

The Backyard Kids actually LOVE reading AND writing.

I'm serious. So serious! What was that? You don't believe me?

We double-dog dare you to start writing in this journal and accept The Undercover Backyard Challenge!! You will see just how much fun reading and writing can be!!

Your Friends,
The Backyard Kids

Undercover Backyard Challenge

1. Devices Down — you can still use devices, just use them less. Think about how much time you normally use electronics (phone, ipad, video games) and cut that in half — OR MORE!

2. Go outside — BACKYARD, front yard, side yard...

3. Read — Write — Move — Have Fun!

4. Complete this Undercover Journal!

Challenge Accepted!

Name:

Age:

LiKes

_____
_____
_____
_____
_____

disLIKES

_____
_____
_____
_____
_____

-Stranded-

Imagine you were banished to a deserted island FOR-EV-ER!!!!

> Banished means that you were sent far, far, far away. To a place that doesn't have many (or any) people.

What five items would you bring with you?

1.
2.
3.
4.
5.

What three foods would you bring?

1.
2.
3.

-Stranded-

List four friends you would choose to be banished to the island with.

1. _____
2. _____
3. _____
4. _____

What would you name the island?

_____

_____

Draw a picture.

5 words that describe you

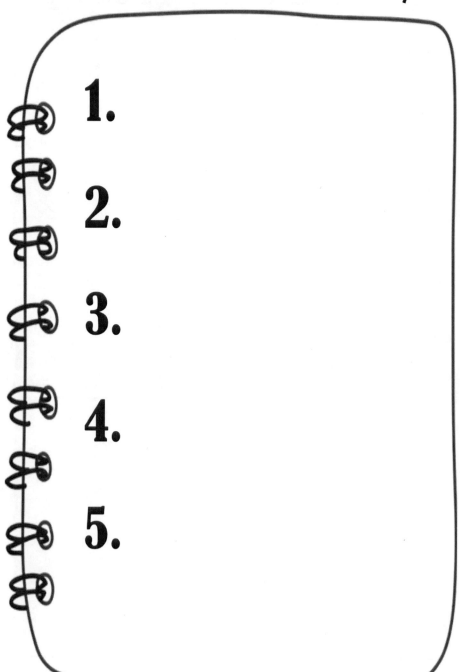

1.

2.

3.

4.

5.

YOU from the FUTURE

Draw a picture of what you think you will look like when you're 40

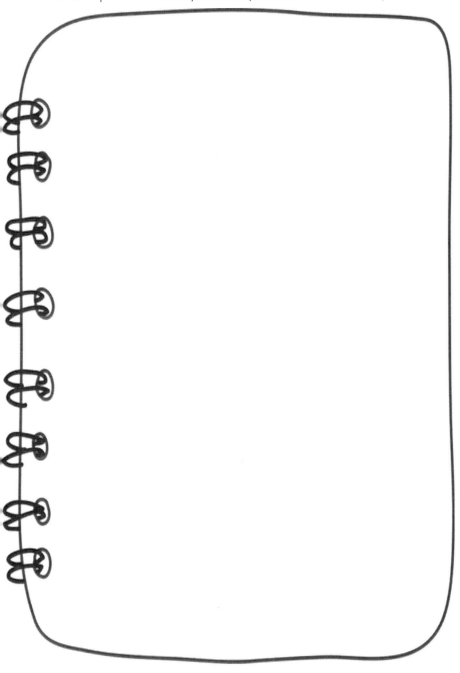

Dream Vacation

Imagine your dream vacation, ANYWHERE!!

Where would you go?

What would you do there?

Would you rather (check ONLY ONE box) . . .

☐ Go on vacation to your DREAM place
BUT with your worst enemy

☐ Stay at home with your best friend BUT your
eyes are glued closed

Oh NO, NO, NO

What is one thing you are terrified to do?

Why?

Terrified means scared times ten million.

Whatever it is, would you do it if someone double dog dared you?

ROLE

Imagine your WILDEST DREAMS CAME TRUE!!! You are the parent... and your parent is now you!

What would you make them do?

I'll go first...

1. EAT ALL THE VEGGIES THAT EVER EXISTED

2. GO TO BED AT 7:00 P.M.

3. CONSTANTLY SAY TO THEM, "IF YOU DO NOT DO YOUR CHORES THIS VERY INSTANT, YOU ARE GROUNDED!!"

REVERSAL

Here's your space to seek parental revenge! Don't worry — it's still TOP SECRET! Let's see what you would make your parents do!

1.

2.

3.

4.

5.

What's on the menu?
Part One.

Rank your favorite drinks — starting with the BEST
1 = BEST EVER …

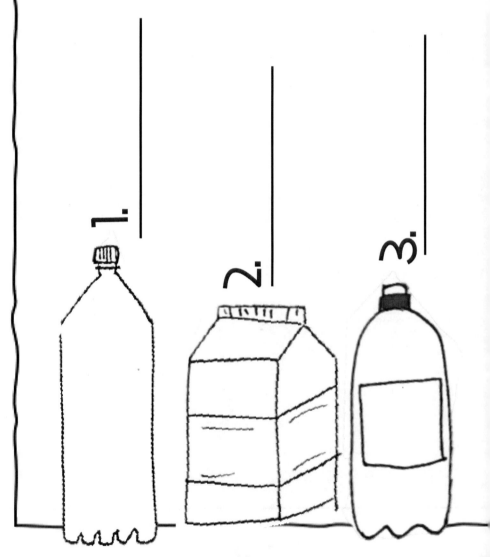

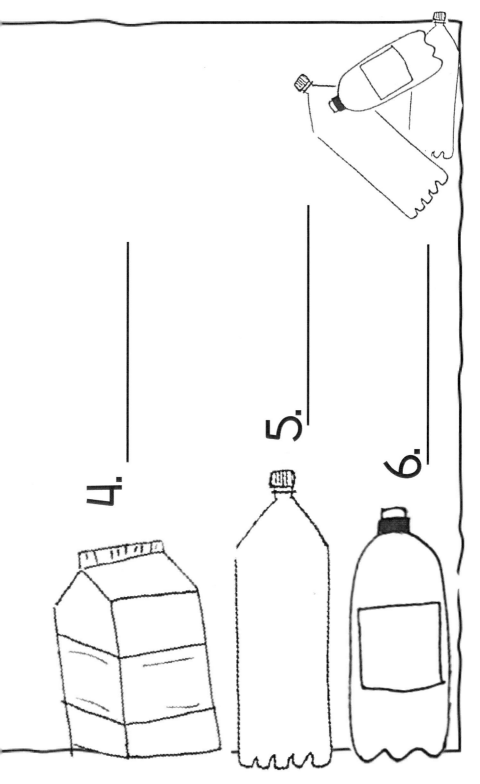

4. _____

5. _____

6. _____

Summer To-Do
checklist

- Have a bonfire
- Go swimming
- Go to the beach
- Take a walk
- Go to the park
- Go to the playground

- Go to a baseball game
- Stay up late watching your favorite movie
- Ride a bike
- Play Marco-Polo
- Run through a sprinkler

Summer To-Do
checklist

- ○ Eat ice cream from the ice cream man
- ○ Play kickball
- ○ Challenge a buddy to a drawing contest
- ○ Have a picnic

Add own ideas here

Would you rather?

Circle the one you WOULD rather do. Good luck, there are some lose-lose situations here.

- Kiss your least favorite aunt on the cheek OR eat your least favorite food?

- Win a dunk contest against the best basketball player of all time OR score a touchdown against the best football player of all time?

- Walk barefoot across broken seashells OR walk with shoes on across fire?

- Have the worst teacher for every subject in school this year OR not be able to taste food for the rest of your life?

- Have a butler OR drive a lambo

Would you rather?

- Win a free 3-week vacation **OR** win front row tickets to your favorite singer?

- Win the baseball championship **OR** skip homework for the rest of the year?

- Eat a pound of dirt **OR** drink a gallon of dirty pond water?

- Have a cat as a pet **OR** a spider as a pet?

- Jump out of an airplane **OR** bungee jump from Mt. Everest? – the tallest mountain in the world!!!

- Skip school for one day **OR** skip homework for one week

Take A Break

What are some of your favorite things to do during school breaks?

1.

2.

3.

4.

5.

6.

7.

8.

9.

10.

WOWZER - that looks like a lot of fun. You sure know how to hang out like a BYK!!!

NEW PLANET

You just discovered a new planet! What did you name it?

_____

Do aliens live on it?

_____

Color in your new planet below!

MUSIC TIME

The BYK love music... list five of your ALL-TIME favorite songs.

1.

2.

3.

4.

5.

Draw your dream house

Describe your dream house

1. How many bedrooms will your house have?

2. Will your house have a pool?

3. What about a butler?

4. Will it have a movie theater?

5. Will it have a candy shop?

6. What about an inground pool with a diving board and lights that make the pool water change color at nighttime?

Create your own team

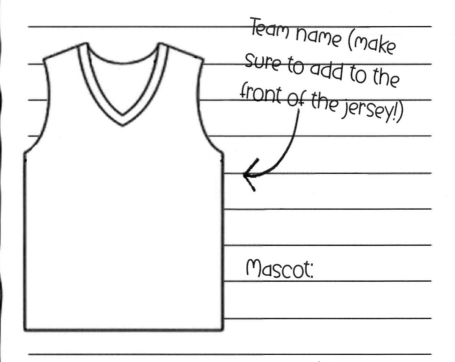

Team name (make sure to add to the front of the jersey!)

Mascot:

Rival team name:

Favorite team song (the one that pumps everyone up!!):

Make up your roster (can be pro's,
teammates of yours, or totally made up!!)

1.
2.
3.
4.

5.
6.
7.
8.

Make sure to add
your last name or
nickname to the
back with your
favorite number
too!!

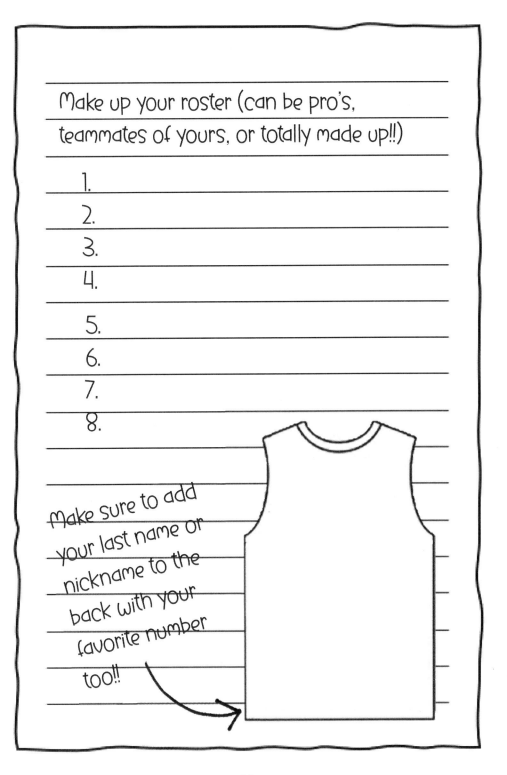

PRINCIPAL FOR THE DAY

Imagine you are principal for the day, what would you allow and what would you ban?

	ALLOW	BAN
1. gum		
2. music during class		
3. hats		
4. science class		
5. ice cream at lunch		
6. TVs in the bathroom		
7. Math class		
8. Homework		
9. No exams		
10. Recess		
11. After school sports		

What four rules would you create for
the day to make you the most EPIC
principal in your schools' history!

1.

2.

3.

4.

ROAD TRIP!!!

If you were taking a cross-country trip with your parents, what activities would you do to keep busy? Circle the ones you would want to do!

Write in a journal

Take a nap

Play eye spy

Watch a movie

Read a book

make funny faces at passing cars

Blast tunes on the radio

Jynx everyone in the car... SILENCE

eat candy GALORE

Collect Postcards at every gas station

Make your own comics

MAKE YOUR

You just invented all new crayon colors that have **never existed before!** Write the name of the color on the crayon, then color it in!!

OWN CRAYONS

CHALLENGE

Think of something super funny that has happened to you. Share it below. Do you think it would make Coach Rod laugh?

_____

_____

_____

_____

_____

_____

_____

_____

_____

Back to the Future

You invent a time machine and travel back in time! What year would you travel back to?

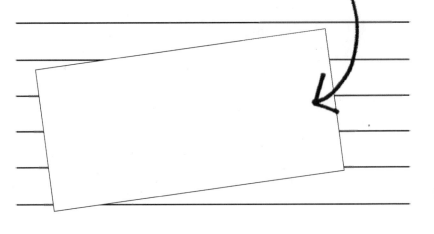

Did you meet anyone?

Draw a picture

How many years ago was 1980?

What year were you born?

Jayden here...

You are amazing!

You are smart!

You are cool!

You made it to page 40

in this journal!

You should be SO proud of
yourself!

Remember: you can do
ANYTHING you set your mind
to!

Positive self-talk

It is VERY important to be kind to your mind! You are special in SO many ways. List 5 things that make you special. I'll go first, you go next.

Me - Jayden

1. I am smart.
2. I have cool hair.
3. I am good at drawing.
4. I hug my mom when I know she is sad.
5. I am a really good big brother!

You - _____

1.

2.

3.

4.

5.

It's MAGIC

You find a MAGICAL seed...

You plant the seed in your backyard.

You water it in the morning before school and at night before bed. You make sure it gets plenty of sunlight. After three weeks of love and care...

What did you grow?!

TIC TAC

Challenge friends, family, neighbors in tic-tac-toe. Keep a tally of your wins and losses in the corner.

TOE FACEOFF

Wins	losses	ties

Sticker Challenge

Create your own stickers by filling in the shapes.

Magic carpet ride

Imagine you have a magic carpet! List
three places you would you take it. Why?

1.

2.

3.

Magic carpet ride

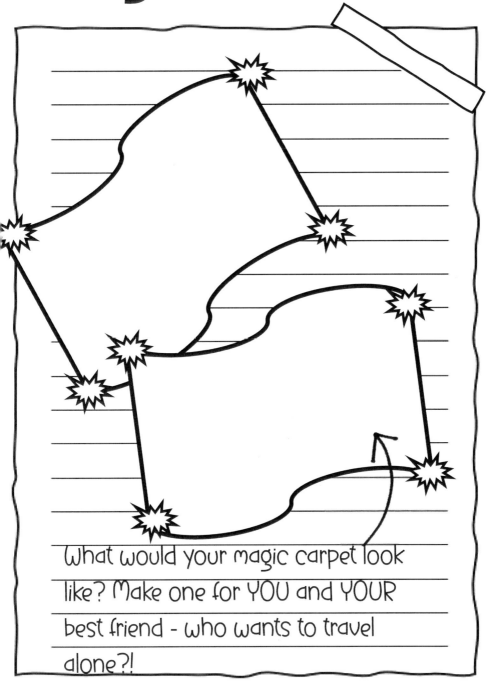

What would your magic carpet look like? Make one for YOU and YOUR best friend - who wants to travel alone?!

TIME 2 CREATE

You are the inventor of a brand-new gadget. WOAH!!

What did you create?

_____

_____

_____

_____

Does it need batteries to work?

_____

Draw a picture of what your invention looks like below.

Does your invention produce something? Does it make life easier? Or does it not do either, but is just totally awesome?

_____

_____

_____

_____

_____

These are a few of

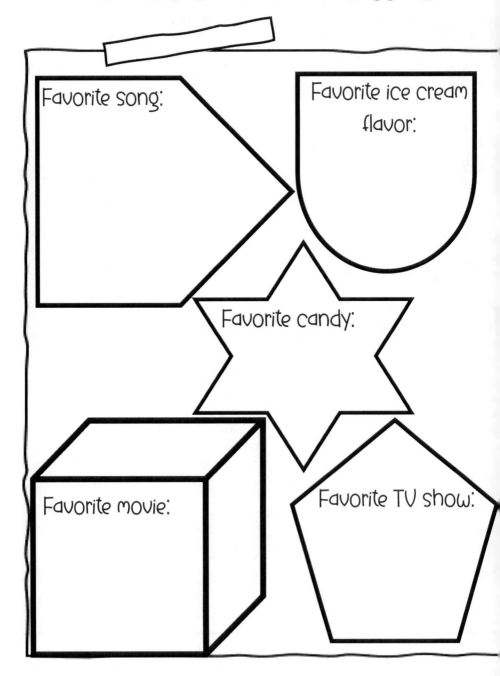

Favorite song:

Favorite ice cream flavor:

Favorite candy:

Favorite movie:

Favorite TV show:

my favorite things

Favorite athlete:

Favorite animal:

Favorite food:

Favorite sport team:

Color this your favorite color!

POP QUIZ

Make a multiple-choice quiz on your favorite topic. It can be about sports, movies, tv shows, books. WHATEVER. After all, you are the teacher! Quiz someone in your house, have them circle the answers.

QUESTION 1:

ANSWER CHOICES (make one the right answer and then three wrong options)

A.

B.

C.

D.

QUESTION 2:

ANSWER CHOICES (make one the right answer and then three wrong options)

  A.

  B.

  C.

  D.

QUESTION 3. True or False. Write a statement that is either correct (true) or incorrect (false).

ANSWER: TRUE or FALSE

IF DOGS RULED

Imagine this…

Dogs took over
the entire
WORLD

THE WORLD...

What would the dogs make their owners do?

1.

2.

3.

Draw a picture of a dog! →

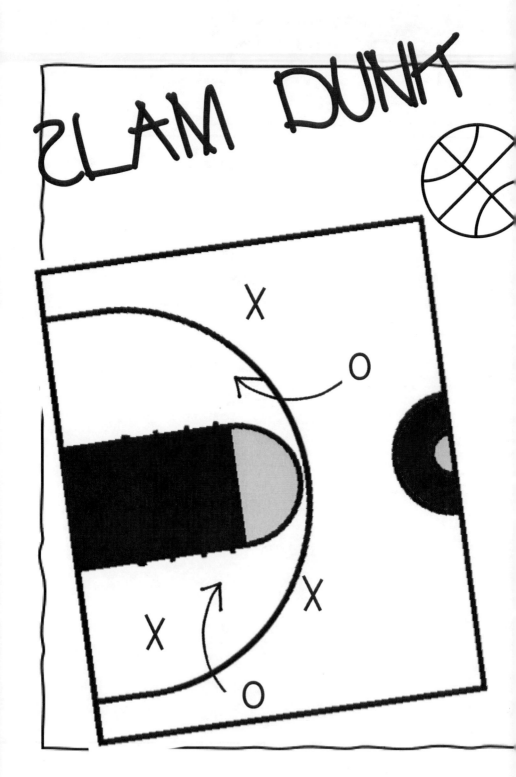

The rules: THERE ARE NO RULES.

- Make your dream basketball team
- Can be a pro, from your own team, from WHEREVER
- You can even go back in time and choose ANY players

ROSTER:

1. Power forward: _____
2. Shooting guard: _____
3. Point guard: _____
4. Center: _____
5. Small forward: _____
6. Power forward: _____
7. Shooting guard: _____
8. Point guard: _____
9. Center: _____

Ha! Ha! Ha!

Ha! Ha! Ha!

Why did the cookie go to the doctor?

It was feeling crumby

Why was Cinderella so bad at soccer?

She kept running away from the ball

What would bears be without bees?

Ears

How do you organize a space party?

You planet ... get it? Plan-it?

Are you laughing yet?!? There are SO
many Dad jokes out there! On the next 2
pages look up some Dad jokes. Or ask
your friends and family to share their best
jokes. Jot them down. Everyone loves a
good joke!!

My Jokes....

More Jokes...

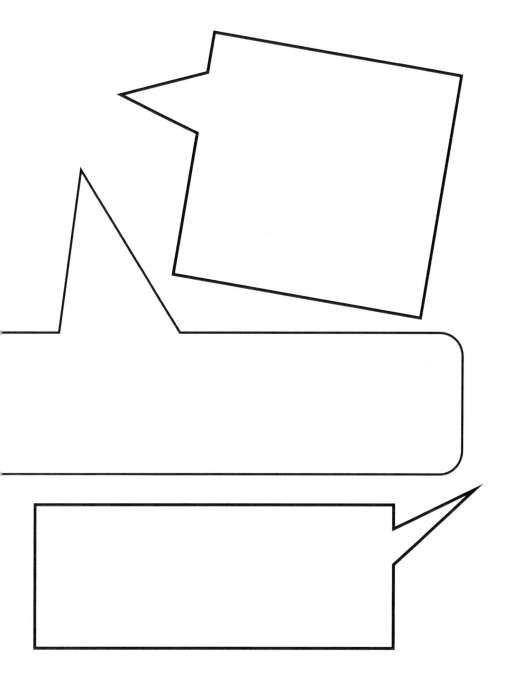

A wishing well is a water fountain that grants your wishes...there is only one catch. You need to throw a coin into the fountain to make each wish to come true. Use the coins below to make your wishes! Do not forget to decorate the coin and write your wish next to each one.

Wish #1

_____

_____

Wish #2

_____

_____

Wish #3

_____

_____

Wishing Well

A note from Ellie:

WOW!!!!

You are seriously amazing.

Halfway there - halfway finished this book.

Do a happy dance and pat yourself on the back!

I made a special certificate for you on the next page.

Fill in the blanks to make it official!

The Undercover BYK Challenge
'halfway there'
certificate

_____

(Your name)

Official seal of approval   _____

Date

The BYK
word search

```
K P R A N K S L L R I N N I N G Q B
I G I S O M E R V I L L E E V P F A
N A S H X X B Q X J A Y D E N B J S
G H W J R G S J M K A J R Z R A Z E
S J A C K M X D B R E N D A N S X B
T G Q P L A Y O F F S I W E Q H K A
O P U E R E L L I E E X S U U B O L
N B K N I G H T S Z K H Q N I R L L
S I S T E R T A K E O V E R N O T B
N M G C O A C H R O D S N F N S E P
O P S S U F I M U S T R I K E H N K
J X B U L L D O G S F O N V G V T V
```

Can you find them all??

Words to Search

Baseball   Kingston

Bash Bros   Knights

Brendan   Kolten

Bulldogs   Nash

Coach Rod   Playoffs

Ellie   Pranks

Inning   Quinn

Jack   Sister Takeover

Jayden   Somerville

                Strike

My street 🏠

Draw a map of your street. Make sure to include any trees, houses, or things that make your street unique!

Make your

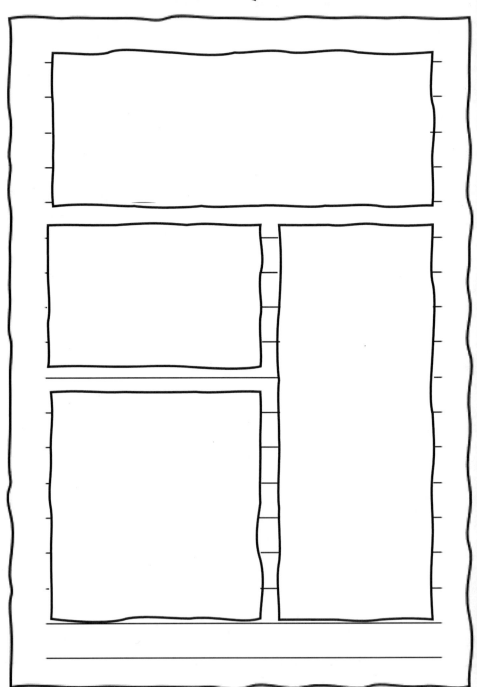

own comic

POST CARDS

You just got back from your magic carpet ride, here is a postcard you sent to a friend or family member!

Decorate the front of the post card and write who you sent it to on the back!

To: Coach Rodriguez
215 Bulldog Rd.
Somerville, 21521

FROM A MAGIC CARPET RIDE

To: _____

You made it to page 76 in this journal!

Now it's time for a brain break!

Brain Break...

Do one or do them ALL — your choice!

- o Play your favorite song. Dance, dance, dance. Don't stop until the song ends!
- o Stretch your arms up to the sky. Count to 25! Do that 3 times.
- o Touch your toes (don't bend your knees) and count to 100!
- o Jumping jacks — start with 10. Do more if you'd like.
- o Go say something kind to a friend or family member.

EXTRA, EXTRA

Make your own newspaper headline!! I'll show you mine!!

COACH RODRIGUEZ WAS SEEN SMILING

This is not a drill...
Coach Rodriguez was seen smiling at baseball practice today. This is a once in a lifetime event! Was it because he ate the spiciest chicken sandwich and had gas pains? Or does Coach Rodriguez know how to smile?
Only time will tell!

READ ALL ABOUT IT

Winner, winner...
Chicken Dinner

You WiN ONE MILLION DOLLARS!!!

How would you feel?

What would you do with the money?

_____

_____

_____

_____

_____

Why?

_____

_____

_____

BYK DRAWING CHALLENGE
→ How to draw Jack

1.	Draw an ear (kind of looks like a diamond not closed, right?!)	
2.	Draw the bottom of Jack's face. Do not forget his ear holes!	
3.	Draw the top of his head, do not forget the eyes!	
4.	Now add his facial features like smile, eyebrows, and nose!	
5.	Nothing left but his hair and clothes!	

Let's see what you got! Draw Jack below!

What's on the menu?
Part Two.

Rank your favorite cereal — start with the BEST
1 = BEST EVER

1. _____

3. _____

2. _____

Have you ever...
- Had cereal for dinner?
- Eaten without milk?
- Used as an ice cream topping?

4. _____

5. _____

6. _____

BYK recap

Make a profile for a friend of family member.

Name:

Age:

Are they a friend or family?

Their LIKES

_____
_____
_____
_____
_____

Their disLIKES

_____
_____
_____
_____
_____

What is your favorite thing about this person?

_____

_____

_____

_____

_____

Describe a memory you have with this person to share.

_____

_____

_____

_____

_____

_____

Giving back

It's important to give back (or donate) to your community! Here are some ideas the backyard kids came up with:

1. Donate toys during Christmas time

2. Help shovel someone's sidewalk during the next BIG snowfall

3. Pick trash up

4. Say something nice to someone or just BE KIND

Prank time

Have you ever pulled a prank?! Did it go as planned? Or did it not go as planned? Draw a picture and describe.

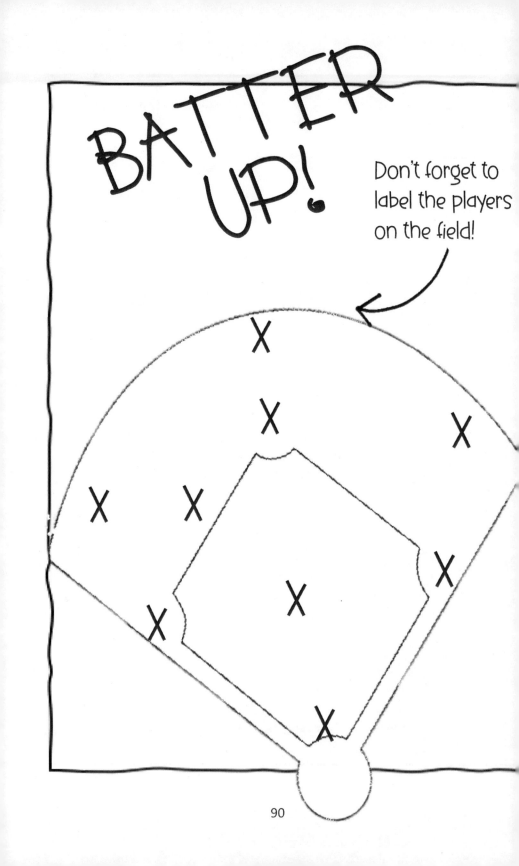

<u>The rules:</u> THERE ARE NO RULES.

- Make your dream baseball or softball team
- Can be from the majors, from your own team, from WHEREVER
- You can even go back in time and choose earlier players

<u>ROSTER:</u>

1. 1st base: _____
2. 2nd base: _____
3. 3rd base: _____
4. Short stop: _____
5. Right field: _____
6. Center field: _____
7. Left field: _____
8. Pitcher: _____
9. Catcher: _____

What's in a name?

Spell out your name, what does each letter stand for? I'll go first.

J okester

A thletic

C ourageous

K ind

Now it's your turn…

Learn American

A B C D

I J K L M

S T U V

Sign Language

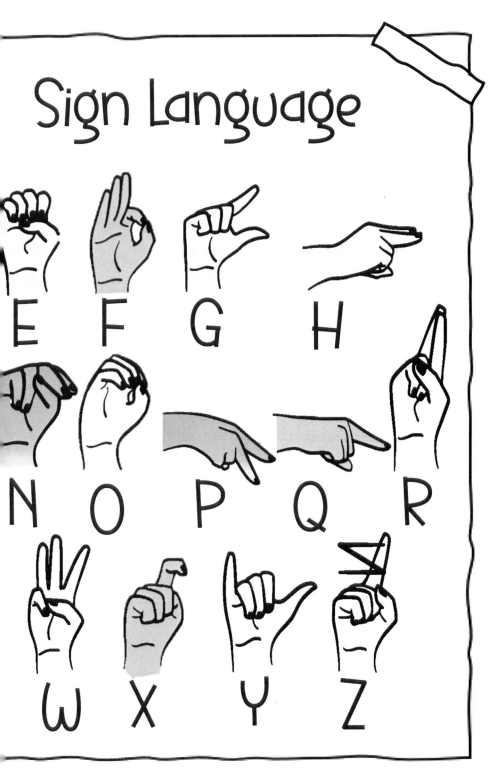

ASL CHALLENGE

Did you know ASL stands for American Sign Language?

CHALLENGE

- Sign your name using the ASL sheet from the previous pages
- Sign a pet's name OR a sibling's name OR a parent's name

___ ___ ___

___ ___ ___ ___

How many books have you read this year?!

List as many as you can...

1.

2.

3.

4.

5.

6.

7.

8.

It's okay if you didn't read any books yet this year! Here's what you need to do…

[1] Skip over these pages

[2] Go read some books,

[3] Come back here to fill in these pages when you finish reading!

My Book Review
Pick a book. Any book.
Tell us if you liked it or not!!

Book title:

Author: _____

Illustrator: _____

Rate the book — color the stars
to show how much you liked it!

☆ ☆ ☆ ☆ ☆

Tell us about the book here…

Bonus points if you draw a picture too.

BUCKET CHALLENGE

Directions: Fill the bucket with goals or experiences that you hope to achieve at some point in your life. Did you know this list is called a bucket list?! DREAM BIG friends.

Check out my bucket entries below:

Volunteer at an animal shelter.

Build an epic sand castle

Learn to ride a bike

Learn how to play guitar

Write your goals here!

To make these dreams and goals come true, keep searching for opportunities! Do not wait for them to just happen on their own! A BYK never gives up...

Name Art

Your name is something really special. It represents YOU and it is something you should always be proud of! Now is time for you to show off your name!

Write your name here:

Do you have any nicknames? Write them here...

Name Challenge: Cover this <u>entire</u> page with YOUR name (or nick names). Marker, crayon, pen, pencil. Write your name: REALLY BIG, really tiny, backwards, in cursive (if you know how), or with your eyes closed.

BYK COVER CHALLEGE

Directions:

- Make your own backyard kids book cover.
- Design stickers for the front
- Make sure to include what edition (is it a sport?! is it about a holiday? is it about vacation?)
- Add your name to the bottom of the book as the author and illustrator!

NEXT: Write your own mini story! Get creative and use that imagination!

the backyard kids

_____ Edition

Written by:

Illustrated by:

A few blank pages coming up... add your own stuff!

Dear fellow BYK,

Congrats!!!!!

You totally tricked the oldies into thinking you were doing HARD WORK!

We hope you had fun. If you have any ideas for our next BYK adventure, ask your parents to send us an email!

Don't stop here though...the BEST part of this book is yet to come!! Fill out your certificate on the next page and then KEEP ON FLIPPING!!!!!!

From,
The Backyard Kids

the UNDERCOVER
BYK Challenge
Certificate of Completion

_____

(Your name)

Official seal of approval _____

(date)

Like I said on the last page, keep flipping, the fun isn't over yet!!

TOP SECRET

the backyard kids™

Undercover

Part 2

THE BACKYARD KID
ART GALLARY

Backyard Kids (just like you and me) from around the country submitted their works of art!

Pennsylvania, North Carolina, New Jersey, and beyond...

Do you want to be part of the next BYK book?
Email: backyardkids215@gmail.com

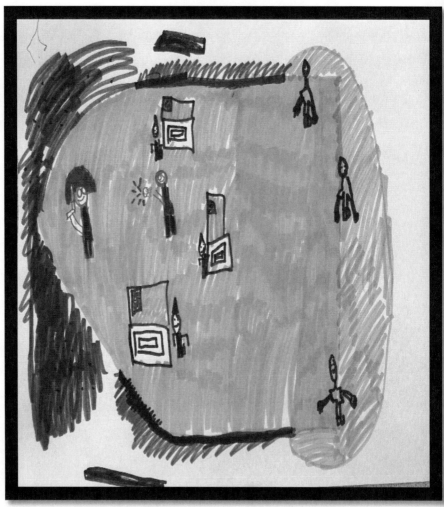

Grady, 7

Jake Finkbiner, 6

Landon, 6
'Music notes'

Chase Finkbiner, 9

Owen, 10
'Space Walk'

Nash, 6
'Spartans'

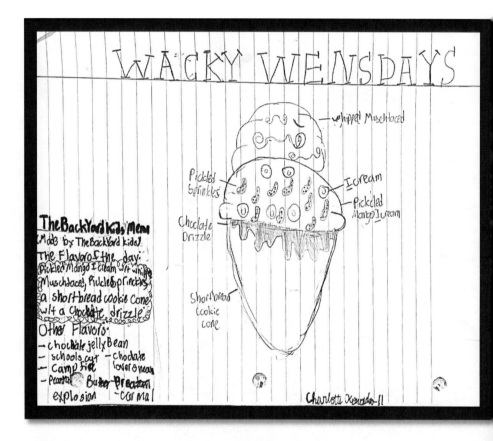

Charlotte, 11
'Wacky Wednesdays'

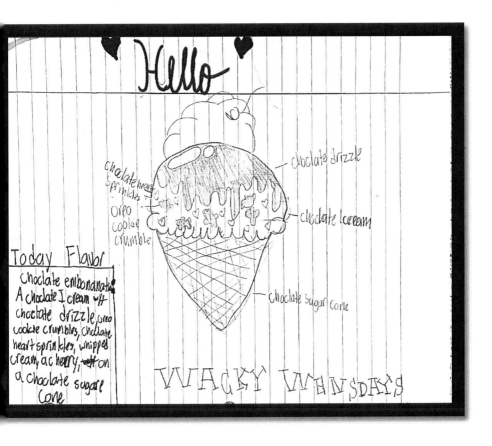

Irene, 11
'Wacky Wednesdays 2'

Brady, 9
'Taking 124 flight'

Luke Sharkey, 10

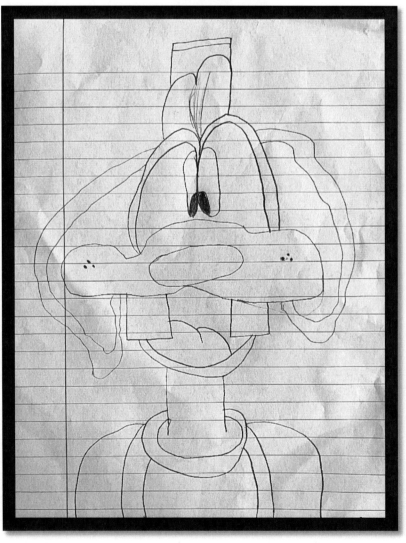

Dylan, 10

Aubrey, 5
'Smell the Flowers'

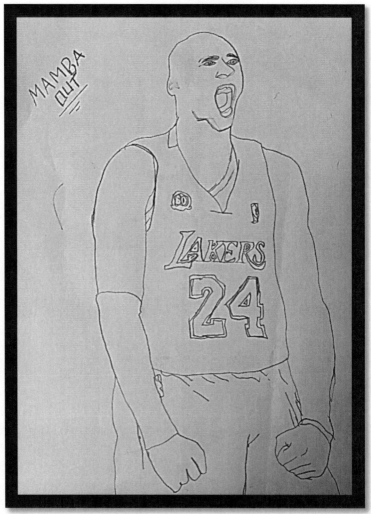

Jack, 10
'G.O.A.T'

Emma, 7
'Play Ball'

Madden, 9
'Home plate'

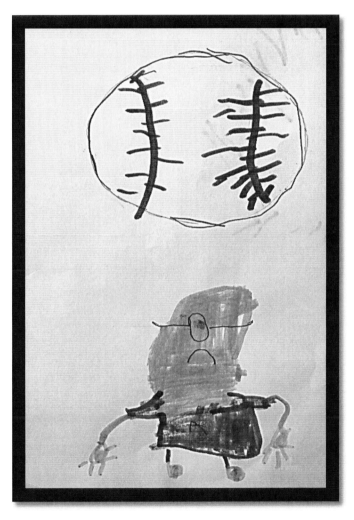

Max, 6

Vinnie Boyle, 9

Ellie, 7
'Always and Forever'

Sean McVey, 7
'Heart of Glass'

Kolten, 9
'Planets and sports collide'

Deven, 4
'Eating a chip'

Braden, 9
'Umpire Jimbo'

Brendan, 5

Ellie & Charlee, 7
'Frick & Frack'

If you didn't make it in the BYK Gallery this time, don't you worry!! Add your work of art after this page.

You can also, email backyardkids215@gmail.com and maybe you could be in the next BYK book!

Let's see it...

BEFORE YOU GO

Did you know, the backyard kids wrote another book? It's an epic story of a baseball team.

We had a wild and crazy season. We even...

Wait...Wait...Wait...

You have to get your hands on the book to find out what happened!!! Smart kid...I see what you did there!

143

Dedication

To our own children! Thank you for inspiring us each and every day!

We love you!

This is a work of fiction. Characters, names, places, incidents, are
either a work of the authors imagination or are used fictitiously.
Resemblance to actual persons, living or dead, events,
or locals is entirely coincidental.

Made in United States
North Haven, CT
16 June 2023

37823257R00088